NEW

HORIZONS

OXFORD

Secular
SATB unaccompanied

— GABRIEL JACKSON —

Yes, I am your angel

Commissioned by The Crossing and Donald Nally, conductor.
The commissioning of the Jeff Quartets by The Crossing was made possible by the support of the Ann Stookey Fund for New Music.

Yes, I am your angel

Kārlis Vērdiņš (b. 1979)
Trans. Ieva Lešinska

GABRIEL JACKSON

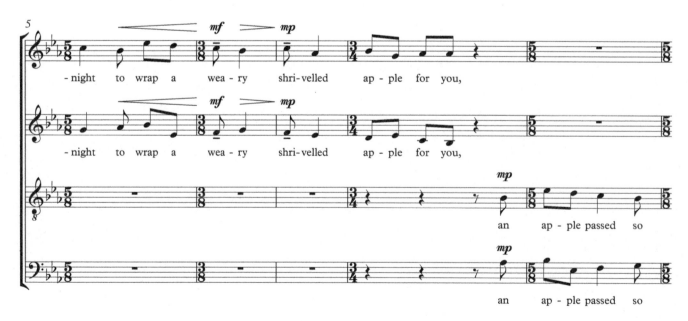

Duration: 4 mins

First performed by The Crossing, directed by Donald Nally, at the Presbyterian Church of Chestnut Hill, PA, on 8 July 2016.

Music © Oxford University Press 2019.

Printed in Great Britain

Text © Kārlis Vērdiņš 2001. English translation by Ieva Lešinska © 2015. Used by permission.

OXFORD UNIVERSITY PRESS, MUSIC DEPARTMENT, GREAT CLARENDON STREET, OXFORD OX2 6DP

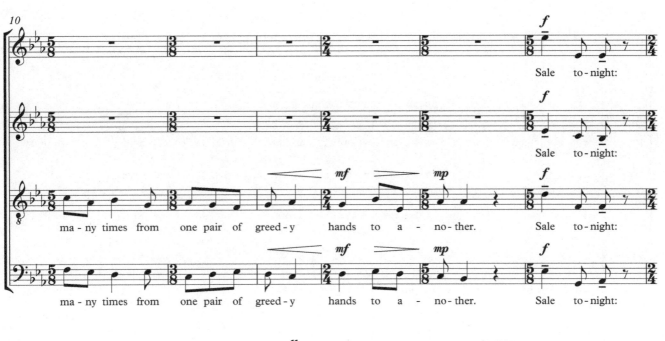

con-tract re - quires; the shift is o - ver,___ in a flut-ter of wings they take off to their

con-tract re - quires; the shift,___ in a flut-ter of wings they take off to their

con-tract re - quires; the shift,___ in a flut-ter of wings,___

the shift,___ in a flut-ter of wings,___

half-emp-ty rooms:

half-emp-ty rooms: cool cradl-ing

___ a nak-ed bulb, a stove in the cor-ner, cool cradl-ing

___ a nak-ed bulb, a stove in the cor-ner, cool cradl-ing

a kiss on that sweet, curl - y - haired head.

hands, a kiss on that sweet, curl - y - haired head. The

hands, a kiss on that sweet, curl - y - haired head. The

hands, a kiss on that sweet, curl - y - haired head. The

gent be-hind you is bu-sy count-ing his mo-ney. He'll buy all the plums and ba-

gent be-hind you is bu-sy count-ing his mo-ney. He'll buy all the plums and ba-

gent be-hind you is bu-sy count-ing his mo-ney. He'll buy all the plums and ba-

-na-nas, he'll buy the su-per-mar-ket per-haps, he'll

-na-nas, he'll buy the su-per-mar-ket per-haps, and I'll be in-clud-ed; he'll

-na-nas, he'll buy the su-per-mar-ket per-haps, and I'll be in-clud-ed; he'll

-na-nas, and I'll be in-clud-ed; he'll

set me on a shelf be-hind glass, dust me off with a

set me on a shelf be-hind glass, dust me off with a

set me on a shelf be-hind glass, dust me off with a

set me on a shelf be-hind glass, dust me off with a

NH225 **Yes, I am your angel** JACKSON

Brockley, April–May 2016

ISBN 978-0-19-341570-6

9 780193 415706